AF316997

THE WILD & FREE ADVENTURES OF VELZY & FIN

GOING SURFING

Velzy and Fin are the best of buddies.

One is a boy, the other is a puppy.

They live in a Bungalow,
where the jungle meets the sea.
Together they are wild, happy, and free!

As the morning sun rises, Velzy and Fin go out to check the waves...
The big blue barrels are pumping out there for days!

They paddle out into the empty lineup, just a boy and his dog.

HEY LOOK!

Here come Mom and Dad going tandem on the log!

Here comes a set!
They paddle, pop up, and surf down the line.

It's all smiles and shakas as they cruise in the sunshine.

Oh No! Velzy had a wipeout!
The wave landed right on his head.

Velzy was scared, but then he remembered what Fin always said...

"Sometimes you fall, whether it be in surfing or life. What's important is to remember that everything will be alright.
When things get tough, be resilient and brave! Remember to always have fun, go out, and catch another wave!"

Now Velzy is ready, he doesn't want to quit.
Another wave is coming,
he paddles and claims it!

It's the best wave of the day! Mom, Dad, and Fin all cheer!

They are so proud that Velzy was brave and conquered his fear.

They surfed all day and
were as happy as could be.

As the sun began to set, a glow of pink and gold covered the sea.

It's time to catch one in, they all paddle with glee...

and catch a

party wave

for the whole family!

As the sun goes down and
the tropical moonlight glows,

Velzy and Fin head back to
the bungalow to wash the
sand off their toes.

All ready for bed, they drift off to sleep to the sound of the waves and reminisce about all the fun they had in the ocean today.

With their hearts full of gratitude and their skin kissed by the sun,
Velzy and Fin dream of tomorrow's wild and free adventures full of surfing and fun!

www.ingramcontent.com/pod-product-compliance
Lightning Source LLC
Chambersburg PA
CBHW042356140726

48196CB00018B/726